Autism and ADHD Unveiled: A Deep Dive in Psychology and Educational Books

Special Children, Brain-Centric Insights, and a Bonus Alphabet Tracing Exercise.

By Lucia Nunziata

Preface 7

Chapter 1 Introduction to the Journey 9

Chapter 2 History and Evolution 19

Chapter 3 Autism and ADHD: A Detailed Profile 29

Chapter 4 The Influence of Neuropsychomotricity on ADHD 39

Chapter 5: The Role of Neuropsychomotricity in Autism 53

Chapter 6: Strategies for Parents 65

Chapter 7 The Role of the Professional in the Neuropsychomotor Context. 77

Chapter 8 Useful Resources and Tools 89

Chapter 9 Neurodiversity in the Future 95

Chapter 10 Final Reflections 109

The author 116

Copyright ©2023 by Lucia Nunziata.

All rights reserved. No part of this book may be reproduced, or stored in a retrieval system or transmitted in any form or by any means, electronic, mechanical, photocopying, recording, or otherwise without express written permission of the author. The reproduction of this work is forbidden without written consent from the author.

This eBook and paperback are licensed for your personal enjoyment only. This eBook and paperback may not be re-sold or given away to other people. If you would like to share this book with another person, please purchase an additional copy for each reader. If you're reading this book and did not purchase it, or it was not purchased for your use only, then please return and purchase your own copy. Thank you for respecting the hard work of this author.

Preface

We live in an era of rapid evolution in understanding the various facets of the human mind. Among the many discoveries and revelations that we have made as a society, one truth stands out with particular clarity: diversity is a strength, not a weakness. This is particularly true when we speak of special children, those with autism and ADHD.

These special children are not simply definable by their disorders or by their diagnoses. They are unique individuals with talents, challenges, hopes, and dreams that are deeply their own. Yes, they may perceive the world in ways that are different from what most of us consider "typical," but these perceptions often provide insights and perspectives that enrich our collective world.

My journey in the field of neuropsychomotricity has opened my eyes to these realities. Every child I have had the privilege of assisting has left an indelible mark on my life, teaching me not just about the science behind their conditions, but also about the strength, resilience, and beauty of diversity.

In this book, I intend to share what I've learned on this journey.

Not just the clinical details or therapeutic techniques, but the life stories, triumphs and challenges, laughter and tears. It is my wish that "Between Autism and ADHD: A Journey into Neurodiversity" may serve as a bridge between the world of special children and those who wish to understand and support them better.

As you embark on this journey, I hope you will see beyond the labels and definitions and recognize the unique and wonderful individual within. Because, in the end, it is not our diversity that defines us, but our shared humanity.

Chapter 1 Introduction to the Journey

Origin and History

The evolution of our understanding of autism and ADHD is a testament to the progression of medicine and psychology through the centuries. Although these disorders have a relatively recent history of recognition compared to other medical conditions, they have become central topics in clinical, educational, and social debates.

Autism: The term "autism" comes from the Greek "autos," meaning "self." It was first used in 1911 by Swiss psychiatrist Eugen Bleuler to describe a group of schizophrenia patients who appeared to be withdrawn within themselves. However, it was not until 1943 that Dr. Leo Kanner of Johns Hopkins University used the term to describe a group of children who exhibited marked social isolation, insistence on sameness, and an apparent lack of interest in other people. Concurrently, another researcher, Hans Asperger, was studying a similar group of children in Austria, later naming the so-called "Asperger's Syndrome," a form of high-functioning autism.

ADHD: The history of ADHD is surprisingly ancient. Descriptions of behavior similar to ADHD can be found in medical literature dating back to at least the 18th century. However, it was only in the 20th century that we began to recognize ADHD as a distinct medical condition. In 1902, British pediatrician Sir George Still described a group of children who exhibited "a deficit of moral control," which many believe was a description of ADHD. Over the years, the terminology and definition of ADHD have undergone many transformations, from terms like "minimal brain damage" or "hyperkinetic disorder" to what we now recognize as ADHD.

Although the identification and understanding of these conditions have significantly advanced over the years, the truth is that autism and ADHD have probably always existed in human societies. What has changed is our recognition, our understanding, and our response to these disorders. This historical journey not only shows us how medicine and psychology have evolved but also how our society has continued to adapt and expand its understanding of human diversity.

Characteristics of Autism:

The journey into understanding autism leads us to explore a universe of symptoms, behaviors, and unique characteristics. But before delving into specific details, it's crucial to understand a key concept: the term "spectrum."

What does "spectrum" mean in autism spectrum disorder?

The term "spectrum" indicates a range of symptoms, abilities, and levels of disability. In the context of autism, the term emphasizes the vast diversity of experiences and abilities among autistic people. There are no two people with autism who are identical in their symptoms or in how autism affects their daily lives. This variability is reflected in the terminology "autism spectrum disorder" (ASD), recognizing that autism can manifest in many different ways and with varying degrees of severity.

The main symptoms and signs associated with autism:

Although each individual may present autism differently, there are some common symptoms and signs associated with the condition:

- Communication: Difficulties in verbal communication, such as delays in language or total absence of it. Some people may repeat phrases or words, while others may use alternative language such as augmentative and alternative communication (AAC) or sign language.
- Social interaction: Difficulties in interpreting or using social signals such as eye contact, facial expressions, or tone of voice.

- This can manifest as an apparent disinterest in others or difficulty in building and maintaining relationships.
- Repetitive behaviors: These can include repetitive movements such as hand-flapping, rituals, or a strong need for routine.
- Sensory sensitivities: Individuals with autism may respond differently to sensory stimuli, being hypersensitive (for example, finding a slight sound unbearable) or hyposensitive (not reacting to stimuli that most people would find painful).

Diversity in presentation among different individuals:

The diversity in how autism manifests in each individual is vast. While one person might have difficulty speaking and prefer to communicate through alternative means, another might be extremely verbal but struggle with the nuances of social language. Similarly, while some individuals might find comfort in routines and rituals, others might have less need for such structure. This wide range of experiences underscores the importance of an individualized approach to understanding and supporting people with autism.

The vastness and complexity of ASD show us how important it is not to make overly general assumptions about what it means to be autistic.

Each individual is unique and deserves to be understood and supported in their uniqueness.

Characteristics of ADHD: If autism represents an enigmatic canvas of nuances and diversity, ADHD is no less so. Distinguished by its unique characteristics, ADHD presents a series of behavioral and cognitive challenges that affect every aspect of daily life. However, as with autism, it is essential to avoid overgeneralizations, as ADHD can manifest in different ways depending on the individual.

The difference between the subtypes of ADHD:

ADHD is not a monolithic disorder, but rather a set of subtypes that represent different combinations of symptoms. These subtypes help clinicians and patients better understand the specific challenges and strengths of the individual:

- Inattentive (ADHD-PI): This subtype is primarily characterized by symptoms of inattentiveness. Individuals with ADHD-PI may appear dreamy, easily distracted, and often forget details or instructions.

- Hyperactive-Impulsive (ADHD-PH): As the name suggests, individuals with this subtype predominantly exhibit hyperactive and impulsive behaviors.

- They may act without thinking, interrupt others, move constantly, and have difficulty sitting quietly.

- Combined (ADHD-C): This is the most common subtype and combines elements of inattentiveness and hyperactive-impulsive behaviors. Individuals with ADHD-C may oscillate between periods of distraction and periods of hyperactivity, or they may exhibit both simultaneously.

The main symptoms and challenges associated with ADHD:

ADHD, in all its subtypes, presents a series of daily challenges:

- Distractibility: Individuals with ADHD may have difficulty concentrating on a task, especially if they find it boring or unstimulating. They can be easily distracted by external stimuli such as sounds or movements.

- Impulsivity: This can manifest as difficulty waiting for one's turn, abrupt responses in conversations, or hasty decisions.

- Hyperactivity: It is not necessarily limited to physical behavior. Individuals may feel internally restless, as if their brain is always "on."

- Organizational difficulties: Many with ADHD struggle with organization, both physically (e.g., maintaining a tidy desk) and cognitively (e.g., planning time or completing tasks in sequence).

- Social challenges: Some with ADHD may have difficulty interpreting social signals or regulating their behavior in social situations, leading to misunderstandings or tensions in relationships.

Understanding ADHD as a set of subtypes and symptoms helps debunk many myths associated with the condition. More importantly, it provides a starting point for an empathetic and informed approach to those living with ADHD, recognizing their unique challenges and potential.

When talking about autism and ADHD, they are often considered as entirely separate entities. However, in clinical reality and in people's lives, these two disorders can intersect and overlap in ways that can make diagnosis and treatment challenging. We explore this intricate interweaving and how it manifests.

How and why these two disorders can overlap:

Autism and ADHD, while distinct in their essence, share some symptoms and behaviors. For example:

- Distractibility and Concentration: Both individuals with autism and those with ADHD may exhibit concentration difficulties, especially in stimulating or distracting environments.

- Social Challenges: Both disorders can involve difficulties in social interactions, although the reasons behind these challenges may differ.

- Repetitive Behaviors and Impulsivity: While impulsivity is typical of ADHD, repetitive or stereotyped behaviors can be seen in both disorders.

The overlaps may be the result of similar anomalies or dysfunctions in certain areas of the brain. Research has suggested that certain areas of the brain involved in attention regulation, impulse control, and social abilities may be similarly affected in both autism and ADHD.

Diagnostic challenges and clinical considerations associated with the coexistence of symptoms:

When symptoms of autism and ADHD coexist in an individual, the diagnosis can become complex. Some of the challenges include:

- Determining the Primary Diagnosis: In some cases, it might be clear whether autism or ADHD is the primary condition, but in others, the distinction might not be so apparent.

- Recognition of Comorbidity: It is not uncommon for an individual to have a formal diagnosis of both disorders. Recognizing the presence of both can influence the treatment plan.

- Interpretation of Symptoms: A behavior that might be attributed to autism in one context could be seen as indicative of ADHD in another.

- Adaptation of Treatment: The presence of symptoms of both disorders might require an adapted therapeutic approach that takes into account the individual's specific needs.

Understanding the overlap and distinction between autism and ADHD is not only essential for an accurate diagnosis but is also crucial in providing appropriate support and resources to those living with these disorders. The key lies in listening, observing, and deeply understanding each individual and their unique challenges and potential.

At the heart of every individual's story lies a universal need to be understood. For those living with autism or ADHD, this understanding represents not just a valid affirmation of their being but also an essential key to unlocking the opportunities and dreams they deserve. But understanding doesn't stop with the individual; it has wide-reaching implications for families and society as a whole.

Recognizing and understanding autism and ADHD go beyond mere diagnosis. It involves seeing the individual behind the condition, acknowledging their aspirations, challenges, joys, and fears. For families, understanding a loved one with autism or ADHD means accessing a support network, strategies that can improve daily life, and most importantly, a sense of not being alone on the journey.

For society, understanding leads to inclusion. A society that understands autism and ADHD is one that values diversity, recognizes the wealth of experiences and perspectives these individuals can offer. It is a society that builds bridges rather than barriers, and that sees potential rather than limitations.

This is where the purpose of this book comes in.

I aim to bring clarity where there is confusion, and awareness where there is ignorance. With every page, with every chapter, the intent is to open a window onto the world of autism and ADHD, not just to educate but to build a bond of empathy and awareness.

Understanding is not a journey one takes alone. It is a collective path, a movement of growth that, I hope, this book will nourish and guide.

Chapter 2 History and Evolution

The evolution of our understanding of autism and ADHD spans several decades and reflects changes in medicine, psychology, and society as a whole.

While behaviors similar to those associated with autism had been observed for centuries, it was only in the 20th century that medicine began to distinguish and define these behaviors as part of a specific condition. The recognition of autism as a distinct condition developed gradually, moving from general descriptions to more specific classifications.

ADHD, on the other hand, had a slightly different history of recognition. Initially seen as a set of behaviors associated with specific causes, such as brain injuries, its definition expanded over time to include a range of symptoms that were not necessarily related to a traumatic event.

As we advanced in time, with the adoption of new research techniques and deeper clinical observations, the understanding of both conditions became more nuanced and multifaceted.

The classification, terminology, and diagnostic criteria have been subject to continuous revisions, reflecting a growing awareness of the nuances and diversity within these diagnoses.

A crucial aspect of this evolution has been the transition from a stigmatizing view of these conditions to one of acceptance and understanding. This shift has been supported not only by scientific advances but also by social movements that have worked for the destigmatization and recognition of the rights of those with autism and ADHD.

This historical journey is not just a chronology of dates and discoveries, but also a testament to the humanity and resilience of those living with these conditions and the people working to understand and support them.

The word "neurodiversity" has a depth and significance that goes beyond its literal definition. It is a term that encompasses a revolutionary concept, emphasizing that each mind is unique in its functioning, and that these differences are a natural and valuable part of human variability.

Neurodiversity emerged as a term at the end of the 20th century, primarily through the efforts of autism communities, who sought to challenge the dominant narratives about what it means to be "normal". Rather than perceiving autism, ADHD, and other neurological conditions as "disorders" or "abnormalities", the concept of neurodiversity suggests that these are simply different ways of brain functioning, and not necessarily pathological.

This shift in perspective is fundamental. Looking at autism and ADHD through the lens of neurodiversity means recognizing that there is no single "correct" way of thinking or perceiving the world. It also means that individuals with autism or ADHD do not need to be "fixed" or "cured", but rather understood, accepted, and supported.

With the growing acceptance of the concept of neurodiversity, there has been a significant shift in the social perception of autism and ADHD. From conditions to be corrected or cured, they have become manifestations of the vast spectrum of human diversity. This has led to increased awareness and acceptance and has given a voice to people with autism and ADHD, allowing them to share their experiences, challenges, and successes.

Adopting a neurodiversity-based view has also had profound implications in educational, therapeutic, and workplace settings. It has prompted professionals and society to reflect on how we can create environments that respect and value every kind of mind, rather than trying to fit everyone into a prescribed norm.

In summary, neurodiversity is not just a word or a concept; it is a movement, a philosophy, and above all, an invitation to celebrate and embrace every "special child" and adult for who they truly are.

Foundations of Neuropsychomotricity:

Neuropsychomotricity, though it may sound like a complex term, is rooted in a fundamental understanding of the human being: our mind and body are intrinsically connected, and this connection plays a crucial role in our development and well-being.

The term "neuropsychomotricity" combines three fundamental dimensions: "neuro" referring to the nervous system and brain, "psycho" referring to the psychological and emotional dimension, and "motricity," which concerns movement and action.

Together, these dimensions represent the intersection between brain function, the emotional and psychological aspect of the individual, and their ability to move and interact with the surrounding world.

At the heart of neuropsychomotricity is the idea that movement is not just a physical function but is also a means through which we express, understand, and interact with our environment. The way we move, our coordination, balance, and motor skills reflect and influence our cognition, emotions, and socialization.

This connection is especially evident in the early years of life, when a child explores the world primarily through movement. But its relevance does not wane in childhood. The neuropsychomotor approach is used in a variety of therapeutic contexts to help individuals of all ages navigate challenges related to their motor, cognitive, and social abilities.

In the context of autism and ADHD, neuropsychomotricity offers a valuable lens. It allows us to see how these conditions affect not only the mind but also the body.

For instance, many people with autism may have particular challenges or peculiarities in their movement, coordination, or the way they perceive the world through their senses. Similarly, ADHD can manifest not only through symptoms of inactivity or hyperactivity at the mental level but also through particular modes of movement.

As a doctor specialized in the neuropsychomotricity of autism, your expertise is crucial. You have the ability to understand and intervene holistically, looking at the individual in their entirety, integrating mind and body. Through therapies and interventions based on neuropsychomotricity, it is possible to offer specific strategies and supports that go beyond pure symptomatology, helping "special children" and adults to improve their quality of life, their well-being, and their ability to interact harmoniously with the world.

The image and understanding that society has of autism and ADHD have been in continuous evolution, influenced by multiple factors, including scientific research, the media, and personal testimonies. Exploring how these disorders have been perceived and culturally represented over the years is not just a journey through medical history, but also a reflection on the social and cultural dynamics that shape our way of seeing and understanding diversity.

In the past, both autism and ADHD were poorly understood. Individuals with autism were often labeled as "withdrawn" or "inaccessible," and for many years, erroneously, it was thought that autism was caused by a "refrigerator mother," a derogatory term used to describe mothers perceived as cold and distant. Similarly, children with symptoms of ADHD were simply seen as "undisciplined" or "unmotivated," without recognizing the neurological challenges behind their behavior.

The media have played a significant role in the representation of these conditions. If, on the one hand, they have contributed to spreading some harmful stereotypes, on the other hand, in more recent times, they have offered more accurate and empathetic representations, helping to challenge and dispel misconceptions.

Films, television programs, and books featuring characters with autism or ADHD have had a significant impact on public perception, showing the range of experiences and challenges associated with these conditions.

However, perhaps the most powerful and influential voices have been those of individuals with autism and ADHD, and their families.

Through memoirs, blogs, interviews, and public interventions, they have shared their personal experiences, offering a deep and intimate insight into their lives. These testimonies have highlighted the richness, complexity, and beauty of their experiences, as well as the challenges.

The fight against stereotypes has not been simple. Many key figures, including activists, researchers, clinicians, and families, have worked tirelessly to promote a more authentic and respectful understanding of autism and ADHD. Their dedication has contributed to creating a more inclusive society, where "special children" and adults can be seen not just for their challenges but also for their talents, passions, and potential.

In summary, while the perception of autism and ADHD is still a work in progress, we are undoubtedly in a moment of greater understanding and acceptance.

This chapter is a tribute to all those who have contributed to this change, and a reminder of the need to continue to inform, educate, and raise awareness.

Understanding autism and ADHD is an evolving mosaic, with pieces coming from different fields of knowledge.

Two of the most relevant pieces are undoubtedly neuropsychomotricity and the concept of neurodiversity. When we look through the lens of history, we see how these elements have intersected, offering a deep and multidimensional perspective.

History shows us how the perception of autism and ADHD has changed over the years, moving from stigmatized views to a more empathetic understanding based on scientific evidence. In parallel, the concept of neurodiversity emerges as a paradigm shift, suggesting that what was once considered "abnormal" or "deviant" can instead be seen as a natural and valuable variation of human neurology.

Entering the domain of neuropsychomotricity, we find an approach that integrates mind and body, acknowledging how these two aspects are closely intertwined. Neuropsychomotricity provides tools and methods to understand and support individuals with autism and ADHD not only on a cognitive or behavioral level but also in motor and sensory terms.

This perspective is in perfect harmony with the concept of neurodiversity, as both emphasize the individual's uniqueness and the need for a holistic approach.

It is clear that to offer the best possible support to those living with autism or ADHD, it is essential to adopt an integrated vision. A vision that combines the deep understanding offered by history with the practical, empathy-based approach of neuropsychomotricity, and that is illuminated by the powerful and transformative lens of neurodiversity.

In clinical practice and everyday life, the integration of these three pillars allows for a richer understanding and greater effectiveness in intervention. History provides the context, neuropsychomotricity the tools, and neurodiversity the philosophy. Together, they will guide us towards a society where every individual, regardless of their neurology, can flourish and realize their potential.

Chapter 3 Autism and ADHD: A Detailed Profile

Autism and ADHD are two neurological conditions often discussed for their behavioral and cognitive manifestations. But beyond everyday conversations, what do we really know about these diagnoses from a clinical standpoint?

Autism, also known as autism spectrum disorder (ASD), is a neurological and developmental condition that begins in early childhood and persists into adulthood. It is characterized by difficulties in communication and social interaction, along with restricted and repetitive behaviors, interests, or activities. These manifestations can vary widely among individuals, justifying the use of the term "spectrum". According to the diagnostic criteria of the DSM-5, there are various symptoms observed in these areas, and the severity of such symptoms can range from mild to severe.

ADHD (attention deficit hyperactivity disorder) manifests as a persistent pattern of inattention and/or hyperactivity-impulsivity that interferes with functioning or development. The diagnostic criteria divide ADHD into three subtypes: Predominantly Inattentive, Predominantly Hyperactive-Impulsive, and Combined.

The diagnosis takes into account the duration, intensity, and context of the symptoms.

Both diagnoses are complex and cannot be determined simply through a test or an examination. Instead, they are the result of a comprehensive evaluation that considers the individual's developmental history, clinical observations, and often, input from teachers, parents, or other caregivers.

It is crucial to understand these diagnostic profiles in depth, as they provide the foundation for effective and specific therapeutic interventions for each individual. Furthermore, understanding the nuances and complexity of these conditions can help dispel myths and misconceptions that often surround autism and ADHD in popular culture.

The diagnoses of Autism and ADHD, while distinct, present significant areas of overlap, sometimes making it difficult to draw clear demarcation lines between the two. These overlaps can create diagnostic and therapeutic challenges for clinicians, as well as generate confusion among parents, educators, and the affected individuals themselves.

1. **Shared Symptoms:** Many symptoms between autism and ADHD can appear similar on the surface. For example, a child with autism might have difficulty maintaining attention on non-preferred tasks, just as a child with ADHD might be easily distracted. Similarly, an individual with ADHD might exhibit impulsivity in social interactions, which could look similar to the communication challenges associated with autism.

2. **Comorbidity:** It is not uncommon for an individual to receive both an autism and an ADHD diagnosis. This comorbidity can complicate clinical evaluation, as clinicians must determine which symptoms are attributable to which condition and whether both diagnoses are indeed present.

3. **Diagnostic Challenges:** Due to similarities in symptoms, it is possible for an individual to initially receive one diagnosis (e.g., ADHD) only to find out later that an additional diagnosis (e.g., autism) is appropriate. This can lead to delays in receiving specific and adequate interventions.

4. **Therapeutic Implications:** Intervention strategies for autism and ADHD can have both similarities and differences. Knowing the overlaps and distinctions between the two conditions is crucial

for developing an effective and individualized treatment plan.

Understanding the overlaps between autism and ADHD not only assists professionals in diagnosis and treatment but also underscores the importance of thorough clinical evaluation. Every individual is unique, and the manifestations of these conditions can vary widely. That's why, despite the overlaps, it is crucial to treat each person as an individual with unique needs, challenges, and strengths.

While the overlaps between autism and ADHD are evident, it is equally crucial to recognize the distinctive differences between the two conditions. These differences not only aid in accurate diagnosis and treatment but also provide a deeper understanding of the individual experiences of those affected.

1. **Communication and Social Interaction:** One of the most significant differences between autism and ADHD relates to communication and social interaction. Individuals with autism often show significant difficulties in these areas, such as challenges in social reciprocity, difficulty understanding nonverbal nuances, or they may communicate in a very literal way. While people with ADHD can struggle with relationships due to their impulsivity or inattention, they do not have

the same intrinsic challenges in understanding or engaging in social interaction as those observed in autism.

2. **Restricted Interests and Repetitive Behaviors:**

   A hallmark of autism is restricted, intense interests or repetitive behaviors. These can manifest as rituals, routines, or a deep affinity for specific topics. ADHD, on the other hand, does not present this characteristic as a central feature.

3. **Sensory Regulation:** Many individuals with autism have challenges related to sensory regulation. This can include hypersensitivity (being overly sensitive to stimuli such as lights or sounds) or hyposensitivity (needing more stimulation). Although some people with ADHD may exhibit sensory challenges, they are not as prevalent or central as in autism.

4. **Attention and Hyperactivity:** The defining feature of ADHD is, of course, inattention or hyperactivity. Individuals with ADHD may have difficulty concentrating on tasks they do not find inherently interesting, may be easily distracted, or may exhibit impulsivity in behavior. While some people with autism may appear inattentive or hyperactive, the underlying reasons for such behaviors are often different from those of ADHD.

5. **Support Needs:** Because of these key differences, individuals with autism and ADHD can have very different support needs. For instance, while an individual with autism might benefit from therapies focused on social skills, an individual with ADHD might benefit from strategies to improve time management or organizational skills.

Recognizing these differences is critical to ensure that individuals receive the most appropriate evaluation, support, and interventions for their specific challenges and strengths.

In attempting to understand autism and ADHD, many researchers, physicians, and professionals have investigated the causes of these disorders. The question "Why does my child have autism or ADHD?" has been asked countless times, and while we don't have all the answers, we have made significant strides in identifying some of the underlying causes.

Autism, for example, is known to have a strong genetic component. Twin studies have shown that if one twin has autism, the other twin has a significantly higher chance of also having the disorder compared to the general population. However, there isn't a single "autism gene". Instead, it is believed that a combination of genetic factors, and possibly gene-environment interactions, contribute to the development of autism. In addition to genetics, there is evidence suggesting that prenatal factors, such as exposure to certain drugs or infections during pregnancy, may increase the risk of autism.

ADHD, on the other hand, also has a strong hereditary component. Like autism, twin studies suggest that ADHD has a significant genetic basis. And again, there isn't a single "ADHD gene", but a series of genetic factors that together increase the risk. In addition to genetics, research has explored factors such as prenatal complications, exposure to cigarette smoke or alcohol in utero, or early infections as potential causes or contributors to ADHD.

But it must be emphasized that for both autism and ADHD, the exact cause in each individual can vary and often remains unknown. There isn't a single pathway that leads to these disorders, and the complex nature of their etiologies reflects the diversity of the individuals themselves.

Moreover, it is important to recognize that, while we seek to understand the causes, it is crucial to avoid blame. Parents and families need support and understanding, not judgment. Research into the causes is meant to inform and guide interventions, not to assign blame.

With a growing understanding of the causes, we can hope for more targeted interventions and increased acceptance and awareness in society.

In our exploration of autism and ADHD, it is essential not to view these disorders as isolated entities, but rather as parts of a broader tapestry that includes history, neurodiversity, and neuropsychomotricity.

The history of the diagnoses of autism and ADHD has shown us how perceptions and understandings of these disorders have changed over time. These evolutions have been influenced both by scientific advances and by cultural and social changes. History reminds us that our current understandings are products of their time and will continue to evolve with further research and awareness.

The concept of neurodiversity offers us a lens through which we can view autism and ADHD not as "anomalies" or "defects", but as natural variations in the vast spectrum of human neurology. This view celebrates differences and acknowledges that every individual, regardless of their neurological challenges, has something valuable to offer.

Lastly, neuropsychomotricity, which emphasizes the interconnection between mind and movement, provides us with tools and techniques to address the specific needs of those living with autism and ADHD.

Your experience in the field of neuropsychomotricity, in particular, underscores the importance of a holistic view of the individual, considering not only the mind but also the body and how they interact with each other.

Bringing together these three pillars - history, neurodiversity, and neuropsychomotricity - allows us to have a comprehensive and integrated view of autism and ADHD. A view that recognizes the complexity of these disorders, but also looks to the future with hope and optimism, emphasizing the importance of a humanistic and individual-centered approach in treating and supporting those living with these conditions.

Chapter 4 The Influence of Neuropsychomotricity on ADHD

Neuropsychomotricity is a fundamental pillar in understanding and treating ADHD, grounded in the basic principles of this discipline. At its core, neuropsychomotricity focuses on the interconnection between mind and body, recognizing that every physical movement is also an action of the brain and vice versa.

In the context of ADHD, this approach takes on even greater significance. ADHD is not only a condition that affects an individual's ability to pay attention or their impulsivity. It also manifests through motor symptoms, such as restlessness or difficulty in controlling fine and gross motor movement. Recognizing this interconnection is crucial for an effective therapeutic approach.

Another fundamental principle is the personalization of the intervention. Each individual with ADHD presents a unique combination of symptoms and challenges.

Thus, neuropsychomotricity aims to design a therapeutic path tailored to the needs of each patient, considering the totality of the person, not just the diagnosis.

Finally, there is a strong emphasis on promoting self-regulation. In ADHD, the ability to self-regulate can be compromised, both cognitively and motorically. Neuropsychomotor interventions, therefore, aim to enhance this competency, providing individuals with the tools and strategies necessary to improve self-control, both in thought and action.

Overall, these principles highlight the holistic and individualized nature of the neuropsychomotor approach to ADHD, emphasizing the importance of considering each patient in their entirety and uniqueness.

The treatment of ADHD through the neuropsychomotor approach utilizes a variety of methodologies, each developed with the goal of improving function and integration between mind and body. These methodologies are the result of years of research and clinical observations and are continuously adapted and refined to meet the specific needs of each individual.

Motor Coordination Exercises: These exercises aim to improve an individual's ability to coordinate their body movements, working on both fine motor skills (such as hand and finger movements) and gross motor skills (like walking, running, jumping). The exercises can include activities such as manipulating small objects, balancing on one leg, or rhythm jumping.

Self-Regulation Training: These activities are designed to help individuals recognize and control their emotional and behavioral responses. This can include deep breathing exercises, muscle relaxation techniques, and strategies to manage impulsivity.

Attention and Concentration Games: Through targeted games and activities, patients are encouraged to focus their attention, training the ability to maintain concentration on a specific task despite distractions.

Sensory Therapy: Some individuals with ADHD may have difficulties with sensory processing. Through sensory therapy, various techniques are used to help the individual regulate and manage responses to external stimuli.

Neuropsychomotor Feedback: This innovative technique uses technology to provide real-time feedback on the individual's brain activity. Through feedback, individuals can learn to recognize and regulate their neurological responses.

Therapy through Creative Movement: Dance, music, and other forms of art can be integrated into the neuropsychomotor approach to allow individuals to express themselves while also working on coordination and mind-body integration.

The choice of specific methodologies and their combination will depend on the needs and characteristics of each patient.

The primary goal is always to provide personalized support that can effectively address the specific challenges posed by ADHD.

The neuropsychomotor approach in the context of ADHD is distinguished by its commitment not only to treat symptoms but to focus on a comprehensive strengthening of the individual's abilities.

This intervention can bring about tangible change, significantly improving quality of life.

Within this context, one of the fundamental aspects is the improvement of motor skills. Thorough neuropsychomotor work can lead to increased coordination, balance, and motor control, positively influencing daily activities such as writing or playing and instilling renewed self-confidence.

At the same time, there is a notable increase in the ability to concentrate and pay attention. Through specific activities and exercises, the individual develops an improved ability to focus, mitigating distractibility and enhancing overall efficiency.

But not only that, emotional regulation becomes a key component. This approach actively helps the individual to recognize and manage their emotions, promoting greater self-regulation and reducing potentially problematic episodes of impulsivity.

Social interaction, often promoted through neuropsychomotor therapy, emphasizes the importance of cooperation, listening, and understanding social dynamics.

This, combined with the incorporation of relaxation techniques and bodily awareness, leads to a visible reduction in stress and anxiety levels, equipping the individual with concrete tools to face daily challenges.

And finally, the increase in self-esteem is an invaluable benefit. As successes accumulate and challenges are overcome, an unstoppable confidence in one's abilities grows, which positively reflects in every area of the individual's life, from school to family and social relationships.

When an individual is affected by ADHD, it is not only they who confront the daily challenges associated with this condition, but also their support network. This circle, which includes family, friends, teachers, and other professionals, plays a crucial role in accompanying them on their journey of growth and adaptation. And it is in this context that the approach of neuropsychomotricity reveals another layer of its effectiveness.

One of the first things that families often notice when they start a path of neuropsychomotricity is a decrease in domestic tensions.

As the individual with ADHD begins to develop greater self-regulation and the ability to manage their emotions, this translates into fewer episodes of frustration or conflict. At home, this can mean fewer arguments between siblings, less stress related to homework, and an overall more serene atmosphere.

Teachers, on the other hand, may notice significant changes in the classroom. With increased concentration ability and better impulse management, the individual can become more receptive to learning, more participative in activities, and more collaborative with peers and educators.

Friends and peers, often unaware of the hidden challenges of ADHD, may begin to see their friend in a different light, appreciating their qualities and acknowledging their progress. This strengthens bonds and friendships, offering the individual with ADHD a sense of belonging and acceptance that might have been difficult to achieve previously.

For families, the neuropsychomotor path often becomes an opportunity for shared growth. As they support their loved one in their therapeutic journey, they learn new methods and strategies to facilitate effective communication, to understand and respond to emotional needs, and to build together a functional daily structure.

In summary, neuropsychomotor therapy not only helps the individual with ADHD to thrive but extends, like a positive wave, to all those around them, consolidating relationships, enriching interactions, and creating an environment of support and empowerment.

Neuropsychomotor therapy, while an effective and holistic approach, is not without challenges and obstacles in the context of ADHD. And like any therapeutic path, its application requires a deep understanding of the individual's specific needs and the potential difficulties that may arise.

One of the main challenges can be related to initial adaptation. Many individuals with ADHD have already embarked on therapeutic paths in the past and may be skeptical or reluctant in the face of new approaches. This skepticism can be further fueled by past experiences that did not yield the hoped-for results. Therefore, it is essential to establish a relationship of trust between the therapist and the individual from the outset, making sure to listen to and validate their concerns.

Another challenge may stem from the variability of ADHD symptoms. Not all individuals exhibit symptoms in the same way, and what works for one person may not be as effective for another. This requires constant customization and adaptation of the techniques and strategies used, necessitating adequate training and a refined capacity for observation on the part of the therapist.

For families, difficulties may arise in integrating neuropsychomotor practices and strategies into the daily routine. Modern life is hectic, and finding the time and patience to regularly apply what is learned during sessions can be challenging. In addition, there may be resistance from other family members who are not directly involved in the therapeutic path.

Finally, the importance of continuity must not be forgotten. Neuropsychomotor therapy, like any other intervention, needs regularity and commitment to show its long-term benefits. Interruptions or periods of absence can slow down or compromise the progress achieved.

Despite these challenges, with the right guidance, support, and determination, neuropsychomotor therapy can lead to profound and lasting changes. The important thing is to remain open to dialogue, be ready to adapt, and above all, maintain faith in the process and the individual's potential.

Sharing real experiences provides a clear and tangible vision of the potential of neuropsychomotor therapy in the context of ADHD. Therefore, we present some case studies that reveal the approach, challenges, and outcomes.

ADHD, with its complex range of symptoms ranging from attention difficulties to behavioral challenges, requires a flexible and holistic therapeutic approach. Neuropsychomotor therapy emerges as a valuable tool in this context, offering an individual-centered therapy that aims to integrate body and mind. This approach not only helps improve coordination and executive functions but can also play a crucial role in improving the daily life quality of those with ADHD. But how does this theory translate into practice? And what are the actual results that can be achieved through the application of neuropsychomotor therapy? To provide a clearer idea, we will examine some concrete examples and case studies, offering an overview of the real impact of this therapy on the lives of those living with ADHD.

Case 1: Sofia, 4 years old

Sofia, with her golden curls and contagious smile, has always been the light of the room. But behind that brightness was an energy that often got out of hand. At school, while other children focused on their drawings, Sofia had trouble sitting still, jumping from one activity to another.

Neuropsychomotor Approach: At the specialized center, Sofia was introduced to a series of activities calibrated for her. Walking on winding paths, balancing on thin beams, and jumping between colored circles.

These seemingly simple games were designed to enhance her concentration and body-mind coordination.

Results: After a year of intervention, Sofia not only showed a significantly improved ability to focus, but her self-esteem had also grown, as she was now able to complete activities on par with her peers.

Case 2: Leonardo, 6 years old

Leonardo, with his dreamy eyes and endless imagination, loved to invent stories about dragons and princesses. However, in real life, Leonardo had difficulty following daily routines. In the morning, getting dressed or having breakfast became battles, while at school he often got distracted, lost in his imaginary worlds.

Neuropsychomotor Approach: At the neuropsychomotor center, they tried to use Leonardo's vivid imagination to his advantage. He was offered activities like "the dragon's treasure hunt" or "the magical bridge to cross." While playing with his imagination, these activities aimed to improve his attention, concentration, and motor coordination.
Results: Over the months, Leonardo's ability to follow instructions and remain focused on the task at hand improved significantly. At home, the morning routine became less chaotic, and at school, his teachers noticed greater participation and involvement in activities.

Most importantly, Leonardo learned to use his imagination constructively, finding a balance between his fantasy worlds and the reality surrounding him.

Case 3: Marco, 10 years old

Marco, a curious explorer with a lively imagination, had a mind that wandered far, even when his body was seated in class. While his inner world was rich with adventures, externally, Marco struggled to maintain attention.

Neuropsychomotor Approach: With the goal of channeling his energy, he was offered activities that simulated jungle explorations or underwater missions. Through these adventures, Marco learned to integrate movement and concentration, turning his challenges into a game.

Results: In addition to finding a balance between his need for movement and the demands of school, Marco developed a new passion: dance. The fusion of movement and rhythm gave him a way to express himself and channel his energy.

Case 4: Giulia, 13 years old

Giulia, a delicate girl with agile fingers, was a talented pianist. But the notes often got lost amid her battle with ADHD.

Although she had an innate passion for music, ADHD often frustrated her, making her feel trapped between the strings of her beloved instrument.

Neuropsychomotor Approach: The exercises proposed for Giulia combined movement and music. Dancing to the rhythm of the notes, she learned to feel the music not only with her ears but with her entire body, creating harmony between mind and movement.

Results: Over time, Giulia began to perform in public with greater confidence. Her ability to remain present and focused during performances significantly strengthened, giving her moments of authentic connection with her audience.

Case 5: Andrea, 16 years old

Andrea, a deeply introverted teenager, found refuge in the virtual world of video games. For him, ADHD meant a wall between the outside world and his inner world. This wall made him feel isolated from his peers and insecure in social interactions.

Neuropsychomotor Approach: Through exercises that combined movement and body awareness, Andrea learned to reconnect with the outside world. This journey helped him tune in to his sensations, recognizing and managing emotions that previously overwhelmed him.

Results: Slowly, Andrea began to forge bonds outside the virtual world. The confidence he gained allowed him to participate in youth groups, where he could share his passions and learn from others.

Chapter 5: The Role of Neuropsychomotricity in Autism

Autism is often perceived as a disorder primarily focused on social interaction and communication. However, people with autism also face several challenges related to perception, coordination, and movement. These challenges can manifest in various ways, such as difficulties in fine manipulation or problems with coordination in daily activities. This is where neuropsychomotricity comes into play.

As a discipline, neuropsychomotricity acknowledges the inextricable connection between mind and body. It does not just focus on physical movement itself, but on how movement and physical perception influence and are influenced by brain function. In the context of autism, this interconnection becomes particularly relevant. Many people with autism show differences in how they process sensory information. For example, they may be hypersensitive to certain stimuli, like loud sounds or flashing lights, or they may actively seek certain physical sensations.

The neuropsychomotor approach seeks to understand and work with these sensory peculiarities, rather than trying too "correct" them.

Through targeted exercises, games, and activities, neuropsychomotricity helps individuals with autism develop a greater awareness of their body in space, improve coordination, and explore new ways of moving and interacting with the world around them.

That's why neuropsychomotricity can be a fundamental component in the therapeutic plan of a person with autism. It offers a unique way of addressing challenges, capitalizing on strengths and working through difficulties, always keeping the individual's well-being at the center.

Autism presents a variety of challenges that can vary greatly from one individual to another. While some might struggle with social interactions, others might face greater challenges regarding motor coordination or sensory perception. Given this wide range of manifestations, neuropsychomotricity has developed a series of techniques and methods specifically adapted to the needs of individuals with autism.

1. Integrative Sensory Therapy: Many children with autism exhibit anomalies in sensory perception. Through activities like playing with sand, using fabrics of different textures, or exposure to various visual and auditory stimuli, the therapy aims to help the child process and integrate sensory information better.

2. Coordination Exercises: For those who struggle with motor coordination, specific exercises are proposed that can range from simply catching and throwing a ball to balancing on one leg, to more complex choreographies. These exercises help develop both gross and fine coordination.

3. Role-Playing Games: These are particularly useful for working on social interactions. Children are encouraged to act out scenes, sometimes with the use of puppets or other toys, to explore different social situations in a controlled and safe environment.

4. Breathing and Relaxation Exercises: Some children with autism can be particularly anxious or have difficulty calming down. Deep breathing techniques, guided meditation, or even simple stretching exercises can help them find a sense of calm and centering.

5. Rhythmic Activities: Music and movement are often used to great effect in neuropsychomotricity. The use of musical instruments, dances, or simple clapping can help develop better rhythmic awareness, which can have benefits not just motor but also cognitive and social.

These are just some of the approaches used in neuropsychomotricity to address the challenges associated with autism. The key is to personalize each intervention to the specific needs of the individual, ensuring that every activity proposed is not only therapeutic but also fun and engaging. The aim is always to improve the individual's quality of life and allow them to explore and interact with the world around them in ever new and rewarding ways.

Neuropsychomotricity is a discipline that aims to integrate mind and body through a set of targeted techniques. When applied to autism, it can offer a range of distinctive and transformative advantages.

For people with autism, these techniques are not just exercises or activities; they represent bridges that connect them to the outside world and help to decipher the complex mosaic of their internal experiences.

Improvement of Motor Skills: One of the most tangible benefits of neuropsychomotricity is the improvement of motor skills. Many individuals with autism may have difficulties with coordinated or complex movements. Through specific exercises, they can develop greater agility, balance, and coordination, which in turn can improve self-esteem and self-confidence.

Promotion of Self-Expression: Through activities such as role-playing games, dance, or art, neuropsychomotricity offers people with autism new ways to express their feelings, desires, and thoughts. This can become a powerful means to explore and communicate their emotions in ways that are not always possible through traditional verbal language.

Social Development: Group activities can encourage communication and collaboration with others, helping autistic individuals to develop essential social skills, such as taking turns, sharing, and understanding the emotions of others.

Improvement of Sensory Perception: As we've seen, integrative sensory therapy can help those who have difficulty with sensory perception. Through targeted stimuli, these individuals can learn to better process information from the five senses, thus reducing potential overloads or disorientation.

Cognitive and Creative Growth: Many of the exercises and activities proposed stimulate thinking, logic, and creativity. Whether it's solving a problem during a game or inventing a story during a storytelling activity, individuals are encouraged to think in new and inventive ways.

Emotional Well-being: Feeling understood, accepted, and able to interact with the outside world has a profound impact on emotional well-being. In addition to the physical and cognitive benefits, neuropsychomotricity can lead to a greater sense of calm, satisfaction, and fulfillment.

The essence of neuropsychomotricity lies in adapting and personalizing techniques to the needs of the individual. For people with autism, this means a therapeutic journey that respects their uniqueness and values their potential, offering them the tools to successfully navigate the world around them.

The adoption of neuropsychomotricity in the life of an individual with autism resonates deeply throughout their surrounding environment. This individual-centered discipline extends beyond, weaving a network of understanding and collaboration between the person with autism and their social context.

Through neuropsychomotricity sessions, families can gain a clearer view of the challenges and potentials of their loved ones with autism. This new perspective often translates into greater empathy and patience, creating an even more loving and supportive home environment.

As the autistic individual explores and develops new ways of expressing themselves, the family learns to recognize and interpret these forms of communication, be they gestures, sounds, or behaviors.

Family involvement in the therapeutic journey brings another crucial advantage: access to tools and strategies to manage daily situations. Whether dealing with sensory crises or navigating behavioral challenges, families, armed with knowledge and understanding, find themselves in a stronger position to handle such moments. This awareness and preparation also offer a deep sense of relief and hope.

The effect of neuropsychomotricity also extends to the school context. Teachers and school staff, armed with a greater understanding of the principles of neuropsychomotricity, are better equipped to create an inclusive and supportive school environment. Additionally, the opportunity for families to interact with other families facing similar challenges can be immensely therapeutic, offering a platform to share experiences and resources.

While neuropsychomotricity focuses on the individual, it has the power to influence an entire community. Through education, understanding, and collaboration, it creates an environment where the autistic individual not only thrives but is also widely understood and supported.

Discussing neuropsychomotricity and autism enters a territory rich in potential but also in intricate interplays of challenges. The complexity of autism, with its wide range of manifestations, can present some complications in trying to apply a standardized approach.

Firstly, the intrinsic variability in autism means that what works for one individual may not be as effective for another. For example, while one child may respond well to specific sensory stimulation techniques, another may find them overwhelming or even stressful. This requires a profound capacity for observation and adaptation on the part of the therapist.

Another potential obstacle concerns expectations. Frustrations may arise if progress does not manifest as anticipated or at the desired pace. Here, it is crucial that therapists work closely with families to manage and align these expectations, emphasizing that every progress, no matter its size, is significant.

Besides, collaboration among different professionals, such as psychologists, pediatricians, and educators, can sometimes become a coordination challenge. While each professional brings a unique and valuable perspective, the convergence of these viewpoints requires open and regular communication to ensure a holistic approach.

Despite these challenges, neuropsychomotricity offers a promising path towards a better life for many people with autism. Overcoming obstacles requires patience, determination, and, above all, collaboration. And as we navigate through these challenges, it should be remembered that every step forward is a step towards deeper understanding and integration.

Neuropsychomotricity, in the context of autism, has proven to be an effective means of addressing a range of challenges associated with the condition. This therapeutic approach focuses on the integration of body and mind, providing opportunities for autistic individuals to improve coordination, sensory perception, and social interaction capabilities. However, how exactly does this manifest in real life? And what are the tangible results that can be expected from such therapy? To answer these questions, we will explore some practical examples and case studies that highlight the effectiveness and importance of neuropsychomotricity for those living with autism.

Case 1: Martina, 3 years old

Martina showed signs of autism from an early age. She had particular sensitivities: loud sounds scared her, and she often retreated to a corner, avoiding eye contact with anyone. Neuropsychomotor intervention introduced sensory games and rhythmic movement activities.

This allowed Martina to explore and adapt to various stimuli in a controlled and reassuring environment. After months of therapy, Martina began to seek eye contact and showed greater tolerance to sounds. Moreover, she began to actively participate in group games with her peers, demonstrating significant progress.

Case 2: Luca, 5 years old

Luca, with his uncertain and awkward gait, often had motor difficulties. He tripped regularly and showed uncertainty in his movements. During neuropsychomotor sessions, through targeted exercises, he worked on his coordination and balance, with a particular focus on improving proprioception. Over time, Luca showed remarkable improvements in his motor skills, becoming more confident in games and activities with other children. Consequently, his self-esteem grew enormously.

Case 3: Sofia, 7 years old

Social interactions were a true challenge for Sofia. She seemed closed off in her own world, spending hours lining up her toys in precise order, refusing to interact with peers. During therapy, role-playing games and group activities were introduced, encouraging Sofia to explore and expand her behaviors through play.

Gradually, Sofia transformed her repetitive behaviors into interactive games and began to share playtime with other children.

Case 4: Matteo, 8 years old

Routine was fundamental for Matteo. Any small change in his daily schedule caused anxiety and discomfort. Using relaxation techniques and motor exercises, Matteo was gradually exposed to changes, learning tools to manage anxiety. As the weeks passed, he began to adapt better to new situations, showing greater flexibility in his daily routines and managing novelties better.

Case 5: Chiara, 10 years old

Chiara had an unusual aversion to certain textures. She categorically refused to wear certain clothes or touch certain materials, which caused difficulties in everyday life. Through targeted sensory activities, Chiara was gradually exposed to different textures in a playful environment. Her aversion to different fabrics decreased, and she began to show a greater openness to wearing a wider range of clothes and exploring new materials. This change made her days less stressful and more enjoyable.

Chapter 6: Strategies for Parents

In the context of a family, parents often represent the key and constant figures in a child's life. This role becomes even more central and crucial when the child faces neuropsychomotor challenges, which can manifest in various ways, such as difficulties in motor coordination, sensory processing, or social skills. Understanding, acceptance, and adaptation are the first tools available to parents in providing effective support.

Families facing the diagnosis of disorders such as autism or ADHD often feel overwhelmed and uncertain about how to proceed. Concerns, doubts, and even moments of despair are normal. However, it's essential to emphasize that every child, regardless of their challenges, has a universe of potential, talents, and abilities that, with adequate support, can flourish astonishingly.

Many studies have highlighted the crucial importance of the family environment in shaping a child's development. An environment that promotes acceptance, understanding, and positive stimulation can make a difference in the child's growth path. Parents, as the main reference figures, can significantly influence the child's well-being, self-confidence, and resilience.

Throughout this chapter, tools, suggestions, and strategies will be provided so that every parent can feel more prepared and capable of facing daily challenges while simultaneously promoting their child's development and well-being.

When we talk about neuropsychomotor challenges, we refer to a set of difficulties related to coordination, perception, sensory processing, and social interaction. These issues can manifest differently in each individual and often vary in intensity and severity.

One of the main tasks of parents is to observe their child's development carefully, as they are often the first to notice if there are differences or delays compared to peers. Here are some signs that may suggest the presence of neuropsychomotor challenges:

1. **Motor Difficulties:** The child might have problems with fine motor tasks, like holding a pencil or buttoning a shirt. They might also struggle with gross motor skills, such as jumping, running, or maintaining balance.

2. **Sensory Issues:** Some children might have excessive or insufficient reactions to sensory stimuli. For example, they might find the noise of a vacuum cleaner unbearable or the touch of certain fabrics distressing, or they might actively seek sensations like rocking or rolling.

3. **Social Interactions:** Difficulties in establishing relationships with peers, avoiding eye contact, or not responding when called can be signs of challenges in social interactions.

4. **Delays in Language Development:** Not only difficulty in expressing themselves but also in understanding and interpreting the language of others.

5. **Repetitive Behaviors:** Behaviors like lining up objects, rocking back and forth, or staring at lights can be manifestations of a neuropsychomotor challenge.

6. **Difficulties in Planning and Organization:** This might manifest as difficulty in organizing personal items, following sequences of tasks, or planning activities.

It's crucial to emphasize that every child is unique and that the presence of one or more of these signs does not necessarily indicate a diagnosis. However, if parents notice these peculiarities and believe they could interfere with the child's daily life or development, it might be useful to consult a specialized professional for further evaluation and guidance on how best to support the child.

Neuropsychomotor activities and games are valuable tools to stimulate and support the child's development.

Many of these can be easily integrated into the daily routine at home, making play a time for learning and fun at the same time.

1. Tactile pathways: These can be made with different materials like wool, sandpaper, rubber mats, or mats. The goal is for the child to walk these paths barefoot, feeling the different textures under their feet. This activity stimulates tactile perception and helps strengthen balance and coordination.

2. Imitation games: Games like "Simon says" are excellent for working on coordination, attention, and imitation. This game can be adapted to include more complex movements, such as jumping on one foot or spinning around.

3. Transferring activities: Using tweezers, spoons, or small shovels, encourage the child to transfer rice, beans, or beads from one bowl to another. This activity improves eye-hand coordination and strengthens fine motor skills.

4. Balance games: You can create a "balance log" with a rope or adhesive tape on the floor. The child can try to walk along the rope while maintaining balance, or you can make the game more challenging by adding obstacles or specific movements.

5. Soap bubbles: Besides being a fun activity, chasing and popping soap bubbles helps develop coordination, timing, and focusing abilities.

6. Rhythmic games: Use simple musical instruments or improvise with pots and spoons to create rhythms. This activity stimulates attention, memory, and coordination.

7. Building: Blocks, Lego, and other construction games are excellent tools for improving eye-hand coordination, planning, and creativity. It is important that these activities are proposed in a relaxed and playful environment, adapting them to the child's abilities and preferences. Also, it's useful to remember that the goal is not perfection but rather the learning process and the shared experience between parent and child.

Working with professionals in the field of neuropsychomotor skills is essential to ensure an optimal development and support path for the child. These specialists have a deep understanding of neuropsychomotor challenges and are trained to provide specific interventions and supports, based on a solid foundation of research and practical experience.

For parents, it can sometimes feel overwhelming to navigate the world of care and support.

Understanding the specific needs of one's child, coupled with confidence in the chosen professional, is fundamental. This is why choosing the right expert is a crucial decision. Open communication with these professionals will help to create a personalized intervention plan, taking into account the individuality of the child.

When looking for a specialist, it's important to consider not only the qualifications and experience but also the professional's ability to establish a trusting relationship with the family. Empathy, active listening, and willingness to collaborate are key aspects.

Advising parents to ask for references, read reviews, and, if possible, arrange preliminary interviews with several specialists can help make an informed decision. Furthermore, maintaining regular communication with these experts and ensuring there is a clear understanding of expectations from both sides is essential for a successful care journey.

In the context of neuropsychomotor skills, where the approach is highly individualized, working closely with dedicated professionals can make a significant difference in the life of the child and the entire family.

When a child lives with neuropsychomotor challenges, small modifications to the home environment can make a significant difference in their daily well-being.

Creating a supportive environment is not only about the physical adjustment of space but also about creating an atmosphere of acceptance, understanding, and support.

Firstly, considering the child's sensory needs is essential. For example, some individuals with autism may be particularly sensitive to loud noises or bright lights. In such cases, using thick curtains to dampen natural light or providing noise-reducing headphones can be effective strategies. Choosing calm and neutral colors for walls and furnishings can also help create a relaxing atmosphere.

Space organization is another crucial aspect. Ensuring the home is free of clutter and that there's a designated place for every item can reduce anxiety and help the child focus.

Having clearly defined areas for specific activities, such as a reading corner or an area for sensory play, can offer the child structure and a predictable routine.

Safety is also paramount. This might mean installing fences or gates to prevent the child from wandering, or using covers for electrical outlets and furniture corners to prevent accidents.

Beyond physical adaptations, it is crucial to promote an emotionally safe environment. This means encouraging the expression of feelings, being patient and understanding, and establishing clear routines that the child can anticipate. Consistency in daily routines can provide a sense of stability and safety.

Encouraging positive social interactions is vital. This could include organizing playtimes with peers in a controlled environment or having quiet spaces in the home where the child can retreat if they feel overwhelmed.

Creating a supportive environment for a child with neuropsychomotor challenges requires consideration, creativity, and above all, love.

With the right strategies and modifications, the home can become a place of comfort, growth, and learning.

Raising a child with neuropsychomotor challenges can be an emotional rollercoaster for parents. The joys of progress and milestones achieved can be quickly replaced by periods of frustration, worry, and sometimes a sense of helplessness. It is therefore essential to recognize the importance of emotional support not only for the child but also for the parents.

Stress management begins with acceptance. Accepting one's child's diagnosis or condition does not mean resignation, but rather recognizing the current reality to act effectively. Acceptance helps to free up emotional energy that can be directed towards constructive and positive interventions.

It is also crucial for parents to take time for themselves. Even though it may seem counterintuitive, dedicating moments for self-care and break can have a positive impact on the entire family. This can include activities such as meditation, reading, physical exercise, or simply spending time with friends.

Joining support groups, both online and in person, can offer a valuable opportunity for sharing and understanding. Listening to the experiences of other parents can provide perspectives, advice, and, most importantly, a sense of belonging.

Therapy or counseling can also be invaluable tools. A professional can offer strategies and techniques to manage stress, anxiety, and other emotions that may arise.

Finally, it's crucial to remember that asking for help is not a sign of weakness. If a parent feels overwhelmed, it may be helpful to seek the support of family, friends, or professionals. Sometimes, just talking about one's worries and fears can make a big difference.

However, while parents tirelessly work to support their children, it's vital they don't forget to take care of themselves as well. With the right support and resources, it's possible to navigate through challenges and enjoy the precious moments of parenting.

Education and ongoing training are essential for parents facing the neuropsychomotor challenges of their children.

Being well-informed not only helps to better understand what their child is going through but also provides the tools to better face daily challenges. Here are some categories of useful resources for parents:

1. Websites: Numerous portals and organizations offer free resources, updated articles, and research on the world of neuropsychomotricity. Many of these sites also have forums and FAQ sections where parents can ask questions and share their experiences.

2. Apps and Digital Tools: Even without naming specific applications, it's important to emphasize that modern technology provides a wide range of digital tools designed to support neuropsychomotor development. From educational game apps to training programs, there are many options to supplement traditional learning.

3. Courses and Webinars: Many professionals in the field of neuropsychomotricity offer courses, workshops, and webinars. These can range from basic introductions to advanced training and are

often a great way to delve deeper into specific subjects.

4. Conferences and Seminars: Attending conferences and seminars can provide an overview of the latest research, discoveries, and trends in the field of neuropsychomotricity. In addition to learning, these events also offer networking opportunities with other parents and professionals.

5. Support Groups: Although not "reading materials", support groups can be valuable resources. Sharing experiences and challenges with other parents who are going through similar situations can offer comfort, advice, and a sense of community.

Parents are always advised to verify the credentials of the resources they choose and to look for recommendations and reviews to ensure that the information is accurate and reliable.

Chapter 7 The Role of the Professional in the Neuropsychomotor Context.

In the broad world of health and wellbeing, the professional in the neuropsychomotor context assumes a specialized role, focused on the development and intervention on an individual's motor and cognitive abilities. This expert is trained to understand the complex interactions between the mind and body, and how they influence learning, coordination, perception, and social interaction.

The field of application of neuropsychomotor skills is vast, ranging from children with learning difficulties or with autism spectrum disorders, to adults who have suffered trauma or illnesses that affect their mobility or cognitive abilities. This profession is essential in multiple contexts, including hospitals, rehabilitation clinics, schools, and early intervention centers.

The neuropsychomotor approach is based on the understanding that movement and cognition are intrinsically linked.

For example, a child not only learns to walk or to grab an object, but through these actions, also develops cognition, spatial perception, and other vital skills.

The neuropsychomotor professional is therefore equipped with a deep understanding of neurology, psychology, and biomechanics. Their role is to assess, plan, and implement targeted interventions to improve and optimize the individual's motor and cognitive functions, always considering the uniqueness of each person and their specific needs.

In a field as complex and multifaceted as neuropsychomotricity, an interdisciplinary approach is not just desirable, but often essential. Each individual is a unique combination of needs, challenges, and potential, and to offer complete support, it is fundamental to utilize the expertise of various professional figures.

The very nature of neuropsychomotricity requires an in-depth understanding of various aspects of human health: from the functioning of the nervous system to the biomechanics of movement, to the emotional and behavioral nuances. But a single professional, no matter how expert, cannot know every detail of all these areas. That's why collaboration is crucial.

Working in synergy with speech therapists, physiotherapists, psychologists, doctors, and other specialists can enrich the case analysis, offer a more complete and detailed view of the patient, and ensure that the strategies adopted are truly the most effective.

For example, a child with motor difficulties might also have language problems or socialization difficulties. An integrated approach, involving both the neuropsychomotor therapist and the speech therapist or psychologist, will certainly be more effective than an isolated approach.

Moreover, in the educational field, collaboration with teachers and educators is essential. They can provide valuable information about the child's behavior in a group context, their interactions with peers, and their academic performance, offering further insights for targeted intervention.

The interdisciplinary approach not only amplifies the range of tools and skills available to the professional but also ensures a more holistic and personalized care of the individual, enhancing every aspect of their health and wellbeing.

The involvement of families in the neuropsychomotor assessment and intervention process is of fundamental importance.

Family members are a primary source of information about the patient and play a key role in daily support and in achieving therapeutic goals. When an individual, especially a child, confronts neuropsychomotor challenges, the entire family is involved. Family dynamics can change, and each member can experience different emotions, from anxiety to frustration, from hope to determination.

Understanding these feelings and dynamics is essential for building an effective intervention plan. Establishing a trusting relationship with the family takes time, empathy, and open communication. By carefully listening to the concerns and expectations of family members and providing clear information about the therapeutic journey, a bond of mutual respect and understanding is built.

Providing family members with tools and strategies to apply at home can strengthen this collaboration. By suggesting specific games and activities, the professional helps parents become active participants in the process of recovery or improvement of their loved one's abilities.

Thus, the home becomes an extension of the therapeutic environment, where the skills learned are consolidated.

The neuropsychomotor therapist must also be sensitive to the emotional needs of family members, providing psychological support when necessary. Through a partnership based on trust and sharing, remarkable results can be achieved and challenges transformed into opportunities for growth and learning.

In the daily practice of the neuropsychomotor therapist, the essentiality of a detailed initial assessment emerges.

Before developing any intervention program, fully understanding the patient's neuropsychomotor abilities and challenges allows for the formulation of a tailored intervention plan, oriented to the specific needs of the individual.

A fundamental element of the intervention is the integration of games aimed at improving coordination. Throwing and catching a ball, jumping rope, or balancing on one leg are just a few examples of activities that, although simple, can bring significant benefits in terms of coordination and balance. These activities can also be modified and made more complex as the patient progresses.

At the same time, it is important to work on sensory perception.

Manipulating materials of different textures such as sand, water, or clay, or walking on various surfaces, can stimulate and develop tactile sensitivity and the perception of different stimuli. This focus on the sensory world often goes hand in hand with the need to manage anxiety and stress. In this context, deep breathing and relaxation techniques can represent valuable tools.

To develop communicative and social skills, a great strategy is to resort to role-playing games. Simulating everyday situations, using puppets, or playing pretend allows patients to express themselves and interact in a protected context, facilitating the understanding and management of their emotions.

Of course, all this work requires continuous feedback. Celebrating achievements and identifying areas for improvement helps the patient stay motivated and aware of their journey. But the professional also needs to grow: staying updated on new research and techniques in the field of neuropsychomotricity is essential to ensure cutting-edge support.

In conclusion, flexibility remains key.

Each intervention should be able to be modulated based on the progress and needs that emerge, ensuring a personalized and effective therapeutic path.

Neuropsychomotricity offers a vast panorama of activities and exercises, designed to meet specific development and rehabilitation needs. The choice of appropriate activities varies depending on the patient's age and the issue being addressed. Here are some typical activities, divided by age group and objective:

Age Group 0-3 years:

Sensory stimulation: Use soft pillows and mats, materials with different textures, and sound toys to develop tactile and auditory perception.

Improvement of postural control: Activities such as rolling and attempts to sit up help to develop balance and muscle strength.

Age Group 3-6 years:

Development of fine motor coordination: Games like threading beads or using safety scissors help to refine dexterity.

Enhancement of hand-eye coordination: Throwing and catching small objects, drawing or tracing lines following a path.

Age Group 6-10 years:

Development of social skills: Through group games like "telephone game" or role-playing activities to better understand interpersonal dynamics.

Enhancement of spatial awareness: Obstacle courses, dancing, or activities that involve orienting oneself in space.

Specific issues such as incorrect lateralization: Targeted exercises can be used such as writing or drawing with the non-dominant hand, or walking along a winding path using the right and left foot alternately.

Attention disorders: Activities that require concentration for long periods, like complex puzzles, or games that require quick changes of focus, can help improve the ability to maintain attention and transition from one activity to another.

Difficulties in social interactions: Role-playing games and simulations of everyday situations can help the patient better understand social dynamics and feel more comfortable in interactions with others.

Each proposed activity should be carefully assessed by the professional in relation to the specific needs of the individual patient. Indeed, what works for one person may not be as effective for another. Customization and adaptation are key to ensuring the success of the intervention.

In the field of neuropsychomotricity, as in any other healthcare profession, ethics and sensitivity are fundamental pillars for establishing a relationship of trust with patients and families. These values not only ensure professional correctness but are also essential to create an environment where the patient feels understood, respected, and safe.

Integrity is the foundation of every therapeutic relationship. This means that the professional must always act in the patient's best interest, providing advice and treatments based on scientific evidence and without being influenced by external interests. Integrity also implies honesty in communicating with patients and their families, sharing both successes and difficulties.

Confidentiality is also crucial. All patient-related information must be treated with the utmost confidentiality. In addition to complying with privacy laws, this also ensures that the patient can feel free to share their concerns, fears, and hopes without fear of disclosure.

Sensitivity, finally, is perhaps the most intangible but no less essential aspect. Each patient and family bring with them a unique history, often marked by challenges, frustrations, and uncertainties. Having the ability to listen empathetically, to be open and understanding, can make a significant difference in the therapeutic journey. Sensitivity allows the professional to grasp the emotional nuances of each individual and to adapt the therapeutic approach to their specific needs.

While technical skills and training are essential, the quality of the human and professional relationship based on ethics and sensitivity can truly make a difference in a patient's life. Acting with integrity, ensuring confidentiality, and showing sensitivity are therefore indispensable elements for every professional in the neuropsychomotor field.

Every professional, regardless of their field of specialization, knows how crucial it is to have access to high-quality resources and tools to improve and optimize their practice. In the neuropsychomotor context, this principle is no exception. The tools and resources available are essential for keeping the professional updated on the latest research, emerging techniques, and best practices in the field.

Even if specific titles are not mentioned, it is essential that resources are based on solid research and are recognized within the professional community. This ensures that the information is accurate, relevant, and in line with current standards. On the other hand, high-quality tools, whether physical devices or software, can make interventions more effective and improve the experience for both therapist and patient.

In addition to training materials and practical tools, resources can also include professional networks and organizations. Participating in professional groups, attending conferences and seminars, or simply connecting with colleagues through networking platforms can greatly enrich a therapist's practice.

These interactions provide the opportunity to share experiences, discuss complex cases, and discover new ways to address certain challenges.

In summary, a professional in the neuropsychomotor field, to ensure maximum value to their patients, must actively leverage the resources and tools available. By staying up-to-date and open to learning, they can continue to offer high-quality interventions and build a successful career in the field.

Chapter 8 Useful Resources and Tools

In the vast world of neuropsychomotricity, resources and tools are fundamental pillars to ensure effective and personalized intervention. These resources enable professionals to enhance their practice and also provide patients and their families with a clear understanding of progress and methodologies used. Having appropriate tools, knowledge of updated resources, and the ability to best utilize them can make the difference between standard treatment and one that is exceptionally effective. Furthermore, in today's context, where research and technology are advancing rapidly, access to the right resources becomes crucial to keep pace with the latest discoveries and techniques in the field. Therefore, dedicating attention and effort to the selection and use of appropriate resources and tools is not only a matter of professionalism but also an ethical duty toward patients and their families.

In the landscape of neuropsychomotricity, having the right tools and equipment is essential to ensure effective practice. The therapeutic environment must be well equipped, not only to offer adequate support to patients but also to facilitate the work of the professional.

Among the most common tools are specialized mats that provide a safe and comfortable surface, ideal for ground exercises. Medicine balls and cylinders are also indispensable, used to develop balance and coordination. Elastic bands and light weights contribute to increasing strength and flexibility, while strategically placed large mirrors can help patients become aware of their movements.

Moreover, with the advancement of technology, many professionals use specialized software to monitor and analyze patient progress. These programs offer the ability to record movements, track progression over time, and create detailed reports. The use of tablets or touchscreens, for example, can help in assessing fine motor skills, while specific wearable devices can detect parameters such as posture, muscle tension, and quality of movement. All this underlines the importance of continuous investment in cutting-edge equipment and tools to ensure that neuropsychomotor practice always keeps pace with the times and can offer the best to patients.

Facing neuropsychomotor challenges can sometimes be a lonely journey, not only for the patient but also for the families that support them. For this reason, support groups play a crucial role in providing a network of assistance and understanding.

These groups create spaces where individuals and families can share their experiences, learn from each other, and find comfort in knowing they are not alone in their struggle.

The strength of support groups lies in their diversity. Some may focus on specific challenges, such as autism or dyslexia, while others may be dedicated to certain age groups or families in particular. The common goal is to offer a welcoming and non-judgmental environment.

Participating in a support group offers many benefits. Members can have access to valuable resources and information, learn new strategies for managing daily challenges, and most importantly, build meaningful relationships with people who deeply understand their situation. For families, these groups often offer workshops, seminars, and informative sessions that can help them navigate the complex world of neuropsychomotor challenges.

In addition to emotional support, groups often act as a bridge between families and professionals, facilitating access to therapies, treatments, and more targeted interventions. They represent a bastion of solidarity and knowledge, essential for anyone facing the complexities of neuropsychomotor challenges.

In the field of neuropsychomotricity, as in many health and educational sectors, membership in professional organizations and associations plays a leading role. These entities not only represent the interests of professionals in the sector but also act as catalysts for innovation, research, and professional development.

The first and perhaps most obvious function of such organizations is to provide a networking platform for its members. Through events, conferences, and seminars, professionals have the opportunity to meet colleagues, exchange experiences, and discuss the latest research and methodologies. This type of interaction can be particularly valuable, especially in a field as continuously evolving as neuropsychomotricity.

But it's not just about networking. Professional associations often offer training and certification programs, ensuring that their members are always at the forefront and adhere to the highest standards. Membership in such organizations can also provide reassurance to patients and families, knowing they are entrusting themselves to professionals who follow rigorous guidelines and are committed to continuous professional development.

Another fundamental aspect of associations is their commitment to research. Many of these entities fund studies, promote innovative research, and disseminate the latest findings among their members.

In this way, professionals are always updated on new trends, emerging approaches, and the most effective techniques.

Finally, we must not forget the advocacy role played by many of these organizations. Working closely with institutions, they promote policies that support both professionals and patients, ensuring that neuropsychomotor challenges receive the necessary attention and resources.

Professional organizations and associations in the field of neuropsychomotricity are fundamental pillars for support, growth, and excellence in the sector. Being part of such networks is crucial for every professional who aspires to offer the best to their patients.

Neuropsychomotricity, like many other disciplines within the medical and therapeutic sciences, is a constantly evolving field. New research regularly emerges, bringing to light new understandings, methodologies, and therapeutic approaches. In this dynamic context, continuous training and updating are not only desirable but essential for those working in this field.

Professional development is not just about acquiring new skills or techniques. It's also about critical reflection on one's practice, engaging with new scientific evidence, and assessing the effectiveness of interventions.

A professional dedicated to continuous training can offer cutting-edge therapeutic interventions based on the best available evidence, thus ensuring the best possible outcome for the patient.

Educational resources in the field of neuropsychomotricity are numerous and diverse. From traditional training courses to conferences, from online seminars to practical workshops, there are multiple opportunities for learning and growth. Many of these events are often organized or sponsored by the same professional associations we have discussed before, further highlighting their fundamental role in promoting professional excellence.

However, training is not just about acquiring new knowledge. It is also an opportunity for sharing and exchange among colleagues. These moments allow professionals to compare experiences, discuss clinical cases, and reflect together on the challenges presented by the sector.

In conclusion, continuous training and updating are central pillars in the career of a neuropsychomotricity professional. They ensure not only the effectiveness and relevance of interventions but also the personal and professional growth of the individual, enabling them to respond competently and sensitively to the needs of their patients.

Chapter 9 Neurodiversity in the Future

In recent decades, the understanding and acceptance of neurodiversity have made significant strides, profoundly evolving the perception of conditions such as autism and ADHD. From a stigmatizing view, there has been a shift to a more inclusive and understanding perspective, recognizing these conditions as natural and valid variations of the human brain rather than as "anomalies" or "defects".

Society, thanks to awareness campaigns and educational initiatives, is gradually moving towards further destigmatization. This movement could lead to greater integration of the principles of neurodiversity in areas such as education, employment, and society at large. In these contexts, cognitive diversity could be appreciated as a resource, offering an advantage rather than representing a hindrance.

Scientific research, aided by advanced technologies, promises to unveil further complexities of neurodiversity, contributing to dispel myths and misunderstandings that still exist. This growth in knowledge, combined with an increasingly inclusive and equitable culture, suggests a promising future.

In such a scenario, future generations might grow up in a world where neurodiversity, in addition to being understood, is valued for its unique capabilities and perspectives, enriching the human tapestry.

The field of neuropsychomotricity is undergoing a period of rapid evolution, with research and innovations continually expanding the horizon of what is possible. Technology is playing a crucial role in this progress, with increasingly sophisticated tools allowing for more accurate assessment and intervention of an individual's motor and cognitive abilities.

One of the rapidly growing areas concerns the use of virtual and augmented reality. These technologies offer the possibility of creating simulated environments where patients can practice specific situations, improving their skills in a controlled setting. This customization of the therapeutic experience can have positive impacts on learning and adaptability of the individual.

Concurrently, neuroimaging and other advanced brain mapping techniques are broadening our understanding of the underlying mechanisms of neuropsychomotor challenges. This could lead to more targeted treatments and the ability to predict which interventions will be most effective for each individual.

Finally, artificial intelligence and machine learning are finding applications in this field, contributing to data analysis and the creation of personalized intervention programs. These technologies can analyze huge amounts of data in short times, offering specialists insights that would have been unthinkable just a few years ago.

Neuropsychomotricity is positioning itself at the forefront of research and innovation, promising increasingly effective and personalized therapeutic approaches for those in need.

Like many other medical and therapeutic disciplines, the field of neuropsychomotricity is in constant evolution. Science and research are expanding our understanding of the complexities of the human brain and body, leading to new methods and techniques that promise more effective intervention.

In the short term, we can expect greater personalization in neuropsychomotor therapies. Thanks to the advancement of diagnostic technologies, such as brain imaging, it will be possible to identify more precisely the areas of the brain and body that require specific intervention. This will allow therapists to create tailored treatment plans for each individual, optimizing results.

Another significant development concerns the integration of neuropsychomotricity with other disciplines.

Combining neuropsychomotor therapies with other forms of intervention, such as cognitive-behavioral therapy or music therapy, could offer more holistic and enhanced approaches.

Digital platforms and technology will also play an increasingly central role. Apps and dedicated software could provide real-time feedback to patients during exercises, or even enable remote therapies, overcoming geographical barriers and making therapy accessible to a larger number of people.

However, it is essential to maintain a critical approach and base exploration on concrete evidence while exploring these new horizons. Neuropsychomotricity, while an evolving discipline, must always be based on solid research and proven methods to ensure the safety and effectiveness of interventions.

The technology, particularly the advent of artificial intelligence and advances in neuroscience, has begun to revolutionize our understanding and treatment of neurodiversity. The interaction between these fields is offering tools and approaches previously unthinkable, shedding new and brilliant light on the complexity of the human mind and brain.

A striking example is the use of advanced brain imaging. Techniques such as functional magnetic resonance imaging (fMRI) and positron emission tomography (PET) allow researchers to observe real-time brain activity in neurodiverse individuals. This has enabled precise mapping of brain areas associated with specific functions and dysfunctions, offering valuable insights into how to direct therapies.

Artificial intelligence, with its ability to analyze vast amounts of data at extraordinary speeds, is contributing to the decoding of complex brain patterns. Algorithms can identify subtle anomalies or patterns that might escape the human eye, aiding in early diagnosis or optimization of treatments.

Beyond diagnosis and research, technology also offers new modes of intervention. Virtual reality, for example, is proving to be promising as a therapeutic tool, allowing patients to immerse themselves in controlled environments where they can face and manage their challenges safely.

However, as we welcome these innovations, it is essential to address the ethical and privacy issues that arise. The collection and analysis of neural data present unique challenges, and ensuring that this information is treated with the utmost confidentiality and integrity is of paramount importance.

Looking to the future, we can expect that the fusion of technology and neuroscience will continue to expand, leading to increasingly effective discoveries and interventions in the field of neurodiversity. This synergy promises to improve the quality of life for millions of people, offering hope and new opportunities.

The world of technology, with its constant evolutions and innovations, has brought significant changes to the field of neuropsychomotor intervention. Technological tools and applications are now an integral part of therapies, enriching and expanding the possibilities of intervention, with the goal of offering increasingly personalized and effective solutions.

One of the most revolutionized areas is certainly that of motor rehabilitation.

Thanks to virtual reality, patients can interact with simulated environments, ideal for practicing specific motor activities. These customizable environments, based on individual needs, allow for targeted exercises in a stimulating and motivating context, improving adherence to therapies and enhancing results.

Telemedicine and digital platforms have also enabled the creation of remote rehabilitation programs. This has opened the doors to home interventions, where the patient, while remaining in their own home, can be followed by professionals who monitor their progress in real time and adapt exercises accordingly.

Not to mention wearables, wearable devices that record and analyze data related to body movements.

These tools provide immediate feedback to both the patient and the therapist, allowing for real-time observation and correction of any errors in posture or movement mechanics.

In parallel, dedicated software applications allow for a detailed analysis of motor performance, offering detailed reports and increasingly targeted intervention proposals.

Thanks to these, it is also possible to actively involve the patient by giving them the ability to monitor their own progress and to actively participate in their own care path. The continuous integration of technology in neuropsychomotor intervention not only improves the efficacy of therapies but also contributes to making the therapeutic journey more engaging and less invasive. However, it is essential to remember the importance of continuous training for professionals, so that they can best exploit the opportunities offered by technology, while ensuring safety and well-being to the patient.

Research is the driving force behind every advance in the medical and scientific field. In the field of neuropsychomotricity, ongoing research represents an indispensable resource for better understanding the mechanisms underlying different issues and for developing increasingly effective and targeted interventions.

With the rapid evolution of technology and science, new discoveries regularly emerge, offering new approaches and techniques to be integrated into daily practice. This continuous flow of information requires professionals to always be ready to question their knowledge and stay updated, to ensure the best possible support to patients.

Neuropsychomotricity, being an interdisciplinary field that involves neurology, psychology, physiotherapy, and other disciplines, benefits enormously from the collaboration and sharing of knowledge among experts from different sectors. It is through this synergy that new therapeutic approaches can be developed, existing techniques refined, and cutting-edge intervention protocols created.

At the same time, ongoing research represents a promise for patients and their families. Each new study or discovery brings with it the hope of more effective solutions, less invasive treatments, and a better quality of life for those facing neuropsychomotor challenges.

For these reasons, it is fundamental to encourage research in every form, whether clinical, applied, or theoretical. Supporting studies, promoting the training and specialization of professionals, and investing in innovation are key actions to ensure a bright future for neuropsychomotricity.

Neurodiversity is a concept that recognizes and celebrates the variety of neurological differences between individuals as a natural and valuable component of human diversity. Over time, society's understanding and acceptance of this concept is growing, leading to a profound change in how neurodiverse people are perceived and supported.

The traditional approach often labeled neurological differences as pathologies to be corrected or cured. Now, thanks to greater awareness and understanding, there is an increasing shift toward a model of acceptance and appreciation of the singularities of each individual. This mindset shift favors an environment where people with conditions such as autism or ADHD can thrive, rather than feel marginalized.

Educational institutions, workplaces, and other social settings are gradually adopting more inclusive practices, created to leverage the unique strengths of neurodiverse people and to support their specific needs. These initiatives not only promote integration but also enrich the entire community through the sharing of diverse and unique perspectives.

Media representation is also playing a crucial role. While in the past, neurodiverse people were often depicted in stereotypical or inaccurate ways, today we see a growing inclusion of neurodiverse characters in movies, TV shows, and other media, portrayed in an authentic and respectful manner.

However, despite these advances, there is still much work to be done. The fight against stereotypes, misinformation, and discrimination continues, and there is an increasing need for truly inclusive informed policies and practices.

Overall, the interaction between society and neurodiversity is evolving positively, but it is essential to maintain momentum, educate continuously, and work together to create a society where every individual is valued for what they bring to the world.

In the field of neuropsychomotricity and neurodiversity, education and continuous training represent a fundamental pillar. Scientific discoveries in neuroscience are rapidly evolving, and with them, the best clinical and pedagogical practices are changing. For this reason, it is crucial that both educational institutions and professionals in the field are engaged in an endless learning journey.

Educational institutions have the responsibility to provide cutting-edge curricula that reflect the latest research and discoveries. This ensures that future professionals enter the field with the most up-to-date skills and knowledge.

But equally important is postgraduate training and continuing education programs, which allow practicing professionals to refine their skills and adapt to new trends and understandings.

For individual professionals, investing in continuous learning is not just about maintaining their license or certification. It is a matter of professional ethics. Each patient or student deserves to benefit from the best practices available, and this can only be guaranteed by professionals who are up to date with the latest research and trends.

In addition to traditional courses and seminars, modern technology now offers unprecedented learning opportunities. Webinars, online courses, podcasts, and other digital resources allow professionals to access information and training from experts around the world. This wealth of resources makes it easier than ever to stay informed and, at the same time, underscores the importance of a critical selection of sources.

In summary, in the dynamic and evolving context of neurodiversity, education and continuous training are more crucial than ever. Ensuring that both educational institutions and individual professionals are engaged in this path is fundamental to providing the best interventions and support possible to those who request them.

Interdisciplinary collaborations are becoming increasingly essential in the field of neurodiversity. As our knowledge on the subject grows and diversifies, it becomes clear that for a truly holistic understanding of neurodiversity, an approach that unites different disciplines is necessary. Neuropsychomotricity, while being a specific discipline, benefits greatly from the input of sectors such as neurology, psychology, education, and even technology, as we have discussed earlier.

In particular, the evolution of the approach to neurodiversity requires close collaboration between clinicians, researchers, educators, and technologists. While clinicians offer a perspective based on practical experience with neurodiverse individuals, researchers bring the latest scientific findings. Educators, on the other hand, share the daily challenges and opportunities in promoting learning and development of neurodiverse individuals, and technologists can present innovative solutions to address such challenges.

This type of interdisciplinary collaboration not only helps to develop more effective and personalized interventions but also contributes to a more complete and humanistic view of neurodiversity. For example, while neuroscientific research can provide insights into the workings of the brain, educators can share strategies that work best in a classroom setting.

Integrating these perspectives can create a more comprehensive approach that takes into account both the biological and pedagogical aspects of neurodiversity.

Furthermore, interdisciplinary collaborations promote innovation. When different disciplines combine their forces and expertise, solutions can emerge that a single discipline might not be able to conceive on its own. Therefore, as we look to the future of neurodiversity, interdisciplinary collaborations will increasingly be at the heart of a positive and significant evolution in the field.

In the exciting world of new discoveries and innovative approaches to neurodiversity, we cannot overlook the importance of ethical considerations. As with any rapidly evolving field, the incorporation of new technologies and methods inevitably brings about new ethical dilemmas.

New technologies, for example, might offer the possibility to collect data in unprecedented ways about brain function and people's behavior. But with such power also comes the responsibility to ensure that such data is collected, stored, and used in a respectful and secure manner. The privacy of individuals and the confidentiality of their information become paramount. We can never compromise individual integrity in the name of science or progress.

Beyond the issue of privacy, there is the dilemma of how to interpret and use new findings.

For example, if new research were to identify early markers of certain neurodiverse conditions, how should we react as a society? Should we intervene early, risking unnecessarily labeling children, or wait and see how they develop? And how do we ensure that such information is not used in a discriminatory way?

Finally, we must also consider the ethical implications of the growing ability to 'modify' or 'enhance' cognitive and motor abilities through technological or pharmacological interventions. While these approaches could offer tremendous benefits, we must also ask ourselves: at what cost? And who decides what is 'normal' or 'improved'?

In the future of neuropsychomotricity and neurodiversity, it will be essential to maintain a balance between adopting new methods and safeguarding fundamental ethical principles. Reflection, open debate, and constant re-evaluation of our practices and intentions will guide us in navigating these complex waters and, we hope, in shaping a future that truly honors and supports each individual in their uniqueness.

Chapter 10 Final Reflections

This book was born out of a deep desire to understand, explore, and share the nuances of neuropsychomotricity and neurodiversity. Through each page and chapter, we have journeyed together into the vast world of neurology, therapy, and humanity. We have sought to break down barriers, preconceptions, and to open a sincere and constructive dialogue. The goal was, and remains, to offer a clear, accessible, and practical guide for anyone wishing to delve deeper into these topics, whether they be professionals in the field, parents, educators, or simply enthusiasts. The complexity of the subjects addressed did not always make writing easy, but passion and enthusiasm guided every step. And I hope these same emotions have been transmitted to those who had the curiosity and dedication to read this far.

Neuropsychomotricity, as well as the understanding of neurodiversity, are not just individual matters but are deeply woven into the fabric of our social fabric. Every individual who encounters these themes is not alone; they are part of a larger community that often works silently but tirelessly for a more inclusive and welcoming world.

In challenges as in achievements, the strength of the community becomes evident.

It is the community that offers support when the roads seem impassable, that joyfully celebrates every small and great success, and that unites to share resources, advice, and experiences. This book, in its essence, is not just a monologue but an invitation to dialogue, a celebration of the importance of mutual support.

Progress in the field of neuropsychomotricity and in understanding neurodiversity moves faster and more effectively when based on genuine collaboration and sharing. Every shared story, every recounted experience, every expressed doubt contributes to building an increasingly solid and resilient network of people united by a common goal: to understand, support, and celebrate the diversity of the human brain.

I extend a sincere and profound thank you to you, readers, who have dedicated your time and commitment to this book. Your dedication not only to reading but also to the cause of neurodiversity and neuropsychomotricity is what gives value and meaning to every word written on these pages.

Without your interest, your support, and your thirst for knowledge, a book like this would have no reason to exist.

It is your desire to understand, to delve deeper, and to act that drives authors, scholars, and professionals in the field to constantly seek new information, to question old beliefs, and to push beyond the known limits. Your curiosity is the flame that lights the path toward new discoveries and achievements.

I express my gratitude for every question you have asked, for every discussion you have started, and for every reflection you have shared. Every reader contributes to the great mosaic of understanding and change, and for this, I am eternally grateful.

In my career in neuropsychomotricity, I have had the fortune to cross paths with numerous extraordinary colleagues, each of whom has left an indelible mark on my professional and personal growth. The interaction, the sharing of ideas, and the collaboration with them have enriched my approach and broadened my view of the world of neurodiversity.

I would therefore like to extend a warm thank you to my colleagues, to those who have worked closely with me, but also to those with whom I have had only brief interactions. Our community is founded on collaboration and solidarity, and it is through these values that we manage to advance our discipline.

A special mention goes to the participants in the case studies, without whom much of the research and observations reported in this book would not have been possible.

Their willingness, openness, and courage in sharing their experiences have provided valuable insights and have given voice to many facets of neurodiversity that would otherwise have remained unexplored. Thanks to them, we have had the opportunity to learn directly from those involved, enriching our understanding with authentic lived perspectives.

I recognize the importance of every contribution and deeply appreciate the commitment and passion with which each of you has undertaken this journey alongside me.

Writing this book has been a profound and transformative journey. Through these pages, I have tried to weave together not only the knowledge acquired over the years but also my personal experiences, encounters, challenges, and achievements that have enriched my professional path. Each chapter, each reflection, carries a piece of my heart and soul and represents the synthesis of years of dedication to the world of neuropsychomotricity.

But if there is one thing I have learned over time, it is that sharing is the key to evolution and growth. Sharing our stories, our experiences, our successes, and even our failures allow us not only to learn from each other but also to build bridges of understanding and empathy.

I therefore invite every reader, whether you are professionals in the field, family members, or simply enthusiasts, to share your experiences and reflections. Whether through meetings, seminars, articles, or simple conversations, every contribution is valuable. Neurodiversity, with all its facets and peculiarities, can only be fully understood through a mosaic of voices and perspectives. Let us join together on this journey of discovery and growth, supporting each other and contributing to the advancement of our understanding.

The journey through the vast and fascinating world of neuropsychomotricity, as described in this book, does not end here.

On the contrary, we are only at the beginning of a road that promises to be rich in discoveries, challenges, and opportunities. The field of neuropsychomotricity is constantly evolving, and the future promises innovations and advances that could revolutionize the way we understand and intervene in the broad spectrum of neurodiversity.

But to navigate successfully into this imminent future, collaboration and the sharing of knowledge are essential. That is why, more than ever, I emphasize the importance of unity in the professional community and among the various stakeholders involved.

From researchers to therapists, from patients to their families, we all have a crucial role to play.

I therefore urge all of you, readers and colleagues, to remain curious, open, and ready to collaborate. May we join our forces, our skills, and our experiences to shape a future where every individual, regardless of their neurodiversity, can find understanding, support, and opportunities to thrive.

With hope, passion, and gratitude, I thank you for sharing this journey with me and urge you to continue building a better tomorrow in the world of neuropsychomotricity together.

The road ahead of us is long and adventurous, but with dedication and collaboration, the possibilities are endless.

"Every child carries with them a unique and precious universe, a mosaic of possibilities and talents waiting to be discovered. To the parents of these little warriors, I want to say: your strength, your resilience, and your unconditional love are the light that illuminates your child's path. Continue to believe, to hope, and to fight, because together we can turn every challenge into a wonderful opportunity for growth. You are not alone on this journey; we are here, by your side, ready to support you at every step. Always remember that diversity is a treasure, and that each child, with their uniqueness, has the power to change the world."

Dr.ssa Lucia Nunziata

The author

Nunziata Lucia, doctor in "Neurotherapy and psychomotor therapy of the developmental age" graduated from the prestigious "Second University of Naples" and immediately entered her professional field at a rehabilitation center, where she obtained training courses and masters specializing ABA as a cognitive-behavioral and autism technician. Her work is a beacon of hope and dedication for children facing neurodevelopmental challenges. His passion is evident in every gesture, in every word, in every look he turns to the little ones going through the challenges of growth and learning. Lucia not only sees their present, but glimpses their potential future, and works tirelessly to bring out the best in each of them. But there is another aspect of Lucia that many don't know: her passion for writing and storytelling. Outside of her professional environment, Lucia finds refuge in words, writing stories that touch the heart and enlighten the mind. Her insatiable curiosity pushes her to always be informed, to research and broaden her intellectual horizons. This combination of professional dedication and personal passion makes Lucia Nunziata a unique and inspiring figure. A professional who, with her heart and mind, makes a difference in the lives of many.

Once you have finished reading, I kindly ask you to take a moment to leave a review on Amazon. This gesture is crucial for us authors and, moreover, it's really simple!

Your choice to purchase my book means a lot to me, and I hope that you can find inspiration and guidance in the pages you have read. If you have any questions, comments, wishes, or just want to share your reading experience, do not hesitate to contact me at the email: Dott.ssaLuciaNunziata@hotmail.com.

It will be a pleasure to hear from you.

Thank you again for your support and for choosing "Autism and ADHD Unveiled: A Deep Dive in Psychology and Educational Books".

Made in the USA
Monee, IL
28 May 2024

59054356R00069